COLLECTED POEMS

◊

CHRISTOPHER OKIGBO

With a Preface by Paul Theroux
and an Introduction by
Adewale Maja-Pearce

HEINEMANN : LONDON

William Heinemann Ltd
10 Upper Grosvenor Street, London W1X 9PA
LONDON   MELBOURNE   TORONTO
JOHANNESBURG   AUCKLAND

This collection first published by
William Heinemann Ltd 1986
ISBN 0 434 53220 7

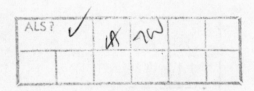

Typeset by Inforum Ltd, Portsmouth
Printed by Redwood Burn Ltd, Trowbridge,
Wiltshire and bound by Pegasus Bookbinding,
Melksham, Wiltshire

CONTENTS

◊

ACKNOWLEDGEMENTS

◊

'On the New Year' first published in *Horn* (1958–9).

'Love Apart' first published in *Reflections*, edited by Frances Ademola (African Universities Press, 1962).

'Moonglow' first published in *Fresh Buds* (1960).

'Four Canzones' first published in *Black Orpheus* (1962)'

Heavensgate first published © Mbari 1962.

Limits © Christopher Okigbo 1964.

Silences first published: 'Lament of the Silent Sisters' in *Transition* (1963); 'Lament of the Drums' © Mbari 1965.

Distances first published in *Transition* (1964).

'Lament of the Masks' first published in *W.B. Yeats 1865–1965: Centenary Essays on the Art of W.B. Yeats*, edited by D.E.S. Maxwell and S.B. Bushrui (Ibadan University Press, 1965).

'Dance of the Painted Maidens' first published in *Verse and Voice: A Festival of Commonwealth Poetry*, edited by D. Cleverdon (Poetry Book Society, 1965).

Path of Thunder: Poems Prophesying War first published in *Black Orpheus* (1968).

PREFACE

◊

THE FIRST time I met Christopher Okigbo at his house in Ibadan, the idea was that we would have a drink and then I would continue on my way. This was 1965, and I was on vacation from my job in Central Africa. My intention was to take the train to Kaduna in northern Nigeria – I forget why. After the drink, Chris invited me for dinner; then it was too late for the train. I stayed the night, and the next day. I was not used to such good company in the Malawi bush. 'There's no hurry,' Chris said, and he urged me to stay for the rest of the week. I did so, and then another week passed. We drank, we roamed Ibadan, we talked about books and poetry. I wrote poetry myself! Another week passed and I thought: A whole lifetime could go by like this.

In a sense, Okigbo's did. He was unconventional, and somewhat irresponsible about petty details, and yet he had a passionate vitality and a brilliant comic gift. The passion shows in his poetry but the humour is absent. He was fascinated by gnomic lines. His poetry is full of them. In an early version of 'Heavensgate' there was a Chinese-looking line that went *etru bo pi alo a she.* When I asked him what it meant he said it was the way he used to recite 'Little Bo-Peep has lost her sheep' in his small village of Ojoto.

He was small, black, definite, and assertive, and he seemed to me to resemble a mark of punctuation – one that is soon to be invented. At the time we first met he was the Nigeria representative for Cambridge University Press, but he was so bored by the job he had stopped opening his mail. It simply accumulated, like fallen leaves. A man came with mail-bags full of proof copies and catalogues, and Okigbo dumped these on a table without glancing at them. They were piled high, they were months old, and many had fallen to the floor. 'There's no hurry.'

His house on United Africa Company Crescent had white rugs and fake-fur walls and white cushions everywhere. Americans told me they hated the decor – 'It's not African,' they said. It looked Italian, like something out of Fellini. It was clean and very comfortable and it was obvious that Okigbo was very happy in the house. He walked up and down, quoting poetry in his odd quacking voice. He had read Classics at Ibadan University. He quoted Virgil, he talked about Palinurus and Odysseus. He was jumpy and highly-strung. It made him a distracted and fitful writer. I think he was too fond of words like 'catechumen' and 'caparison' and 'panegyric'. It takes genius to use such words in any poem. He was at his best and most memorable at his simplest:

We carry in our worlds that flourish
Our worlds that have failed . . .

viii

He was a Catholic, like many other Igbo people; but his traditional gods also influenced him, and he could be plainly superstitious. One day he brought his Jaguar into a garage to have the licence-plate mounted on to the bumper. The mechanic looked at it and said, 'That's an unlucky number.' Chris would not touch the car until he had a new plate. We drove through a storm on another occasion, and when a tree fell across the road, he insisted we turn back – it was a bad omen.

He was not aggressive – indeed, he was very polite. He was a completely independent spirit, one of the freest men I have ever known. He was very loyal to his friends – fiercely so, and this certainty seemed to breed in him a strange stubbornness. Once we went to a Wole Soyinka play at the university. We arrived a few minutes late and as there were no seats – though we had tickets – Chris decided to stand in the middle of the aisle until someone found us seats. People behind us began telling us to move. I moved, but Chris stood his ground. There were shouts. Still, he didn't move. '*Get out of the way!*' Then the disruption was total. The play stopped, the lights went on. Three big men appeared and tried to carry him out. He went limp. They lifted him. He snatched at a door handle. The handle broke, the door smashed. He screamed, 'You broke my arm!' Afterwards he laughed about it.

You can see in his poems how devoted he was to his people, his region, his village. I imagine him to have been the most mocking and mischievous child, one of those high-spirited kids in torn shorts that screech and make the other children laugh. The sort of child who believes his village to be the centre of the world. He was a young man at the time of Nigeria's independence, and still a young man at the time of the Civil War, when he died.

He was an unlikely soldier, but so was Byron, so was Rupert Brooke, so were many of the classical poet-heroes that Okigbo idolized. People believed that the Biafran War should not have been fought. But what was Nigeria? It was a jumble of alienated regions. Okigbo would have jeered at the way the country's name had been coined in a despatch by a British woman journalist in 1897. But Biafra was Igboland: one language, one culture, one people. There was every reason for it to exist as a sovereign state. Okigbo did not care for politics, but he was greatly attached to the past and very certain of his identity. He was intelligent, open-minded, self-assured – the sort of person who is thrown into jail in Africa, or is speared to death or deported for being difficult. He was just the sort of person every country needs. Characteristically – in a war that few people here now remember – he died fighting for his village.

Paul Theroux
London, January 1986

INTRODUCTION

◊

CHRISTOPHER OKIGBO was born in the small village of Ojoto in the former Eastern Region of Nigeria in 1932. His family were Igbo Catholics. He attended the local Catholic primary school, at which his father taught, before proceeding to Government College, Umuahia, for his secondary education. The Government Colleges, of which there were only half a dozen or so in the country, were set up by the colonial rulers as the training ground for the future élite. Entrance was by competitive examination, and it is a good indication of his early scholastic abilities that he distinguished himself while he was there, obtaining Grade One in his Cambridge School Certificate with distinction in his favourite subjects, mathematics, literature, Latin and music. In 1951 he was admitted into the University College, Ibadan, where he read Classics. It was at Ibadan that he published his first attempts at poetry, 'On the New Year' and 'Debtor's Lane'. Both these poems appeared in a student literary magazine, *The Horn*, edited by his friend and fellow-writer, J.P. Clark, but it wasn't until 1958, two years after he graduated, that he began to think of poetry as his vocation:

> There wasn't a stage when I decided that I definitely wished to be a poet; there was a stage when I found that I couldn't be anything else. And I think that the turning point came in December 1958, when I knew that I couldn't be anything else than a poet. It's just like somebody who receives a call in the middle of the night to religious service, in order to become a priest of a particular cult, and I didn't have any choice in the matter. I just had to obey.

In the meantime he had to make a living. For the next nine years he took up and abandoned an extraordinary diversity of occupations: company executive, secondary school teacher, university librarian, publisher's representative, businessman. This was in keeping with the picture of an 'energetic, restless man, fully charged with life'.[2] The words are those of J.P. Clark, who knew him as well as anybody, and they are confirmed by the critic Sunday Anozie, who has written the only full-length study of Okigbo to date.[3] As a businessman he was apparently a complete failure. Anozie refers to a certain Italian contract financier with whom Okigbo stayed for a while in Lagos in 1966 as an erstwhile partner, but nothing much seems to have come of it. Clark, who visited Okigbo at the time, remembers a lot of excited talk far into the night on matters of high finance, but he remained sceptical. In any case events in the country soon changed whatever plans he did have.

Nigeria had been granted independence in 1960.

Within four years there was a crisis in the former Western Region as accusations of ballot-rigging and large-scale corruption were levelled against the government. The leader of the Opposition was thrown into prison and a reign of terror began until, in January 1966, the army stepped in. If their intention had been to bring some form of stability to a country plundered by five years of irresponsible leadership, they were mistaken. What it did was unleash tribal mistrust, which resulted in a counter-coup seven months later and the massacre of Igbos living in the North. Civil war was only a matter of time as Igbos from all over the country fled home and Ojukwu seceded to form the new state of Biafra. Okigbo, in common with many Igbo intellectuals, joined the exodus, but unlike them he went a step further and enlisted in the Biafran army. He was given the rank of major by special commission and in August 1967, three months after the declaration of war, he was killed in action defending the university town of Nsukka. He was only thirty-five years old, but by then he had achieved the reputation as the country's foremost poet. It is a reputation which has remained intact to the present day. One can gauge how highly his fellow-writers regard him by the number of poems dedicated to his memory. The bulk of them, thirty-four in all by thirty different contributors, have been collected in a small anthology co-edited by his friend and contemporary at Ibadan, the novelist Chinua Achebe.[4]

These simple facts hide what was a complex fate, the fate of a man set apart from his society by the circumstances of his life. It was his education rather than his

Catholicism which made this so. As an Igbo Catholic he wasn't unusual. Since the early nineteenth century the Igbos had been particularly receptive to missionary activity. In the first place Christianity was never construed as a threat to the indigenous religion, which was far from hostile to alternative views of the universe. Secondly, Igbo society was profoundly republican. They had no kings or chiefs. This made for an open society in which birth counted for very little: a man was judged by what he achieved through his own exertions. Joining the Church gave access to literacy through the mission schools, and literacy was the source of the new power.

His education was a different matter. At the University College he was one of less than a thousand students in the country's only institution of higher learning. The existence of an educated élite was not a new phenomenon by any means. Nigerians had been going abroad for further studies since the turn of the century, but they had always represented a tiny minority who invariably found themselves in a peculiar position in relation both to their uneducated compatriots and their colonial masters. Where, precisely, did they belong in the scheme of things? Taught to despise the society that had given birth to them, they were denied access to the society into which they had been educated. They were neither Nigerian nor British; they existed in a half-world, the boundaries of which were unclear but from which there was little escape. Inevitably it was these people who were in the forefront of the agitation for independence. Okigbo was a member of this élite, but the matter was further

complicated by the fact that he belonged to a generation which reached maturity at the same time as the
country achieved that long-desired independence.
This put them in an onerous position with regard to
the emergent state. In an important sense the success
or failure of independent Nigeria rested on their
shoulders. They were denied even the luxury of their
predecessors who could at least comfort themselves
with the knowledge that ultimately they did not have
to take responsibility for a political system they did not
create. It is a sign of the tension that Okigbo's generation lived under that it was to give rise to a wholly new
literature. It is no accident that it was they who,
singlehandedly, put Nigeria on the world literary map.
They were a generation of writers, of whom Okigbo
was only one of many. Before their arrival there had
been no such thing as Nigerian literature in English.
In ten years, between the mid-1950s and the outbreak
of the civil war, there was an explosion of literary
creativity. A list of the writers who began publishing
at this time include many of the best-known names of
this new literature: Chinua Achebe, Elechi Amadi, J.P.
Clark, Obi Egbuna, Cyprian Ekwensi, V.C. Ike, John
Munonye, Flora Nwapa, Nkem Nwankwo, Onuora
Nzekwu, Gabriel Okara, Wole Soyinka as well as
Okigbo himself. They form a remarkably homo-
genous group. With the exception of Ekwensi they
were all born between 1928 and 1938; many of them
went to one of the Government Colleges and later the
University College, Ibadan; and, with the exception of
Clark, Okara and Soyinka, they were all Igbo.

The Igbo contribution to modern Nigerian literature is one of the first things that strikes anyone coming to the subject for the first time, but it is hardly surprising given the alacrity with which they seized educational opportunities. It was equally reflected in other spheres of public life. It was they who, at independence, were best qualified to fill the civil service, the teaching posts, and the upper reaches of the Armed Forces. The irony is that it was precisely the disproportionate contribution they made towards the country's development which was to lead to their troubles. It wasn't merely that the British mistrusted them as they mistrusted all those who acquired an education and were thereby in a position to challenge their authority. It was that the British actively preferred the Muslim Northerners. The Northerners had never wanted anything to do with the white man's education or his religion. The Northern feudal aristocracy had only succumbed to colonial rule on the understanding that the missionaries would be debarred from their territory. The British were quite happy to go along with this. They were content for the feudal structure of Northern society to remain intact because it meant that they could rule with the minimum of force. In any case, they genuinely respected Islam, which to them was a proper religion, unlike the 'paganism' they had encountered in the South: the Northerners were 'civilised' in a way that the Southerners were not. The relationship was so cosy, in fact, that the Northern aristocracy didn't even want independence when it came. They were quite happy to work with the colonial authority for the maintenance of their power, and they knew full well that when independence did arrive they would be at a disadvantage when it came to the nuts and bolts of running a modern state. But they couldn't hold back the agitation for independence, though they did their best to contain it for as long as possible. When independence finally came it was they to whom the British handed over power, but it was the Southerners, especially the Igbos, on whom they were forced to depend. When the army stepped in it was they who were butchered, and on the orders of Igbo officers at that. Hence the backlash, hence the civil war, hence Okigbo's death.

And yet Okigbo was the last man who should have perished in a fratricidal war. Achebe, in his introduction to the anthology already referred to, talks of his 'gift for fellowship surpassing anything I had seen or thought possible. He had friends, admirers, fans, cronies of both sexes, from all ages, all social classes, all professions, all ethnic groups.'5 This is what makes his death doubly tragic: not only was he the most promising poet of his generation, he was also a man lacking the cultural and racial chauvinism that made both imperialism and the civil war possible. This instinctive generosity towards life and people is also the distinctive quality of his poetry. He saw more clearly than most the necessity of separating the facts of imperialism, with its attendant injustices, from the truth of the man it had made him. In other words he no more hated the British than he did the Northerners. In an interview he gave to the BBC while on a visit to Britain he can barely control his irritation when asked about his cultural allegiance:

I think that it is a lot of nonsense talk all this we hear nowadays of men of two worlds. I belong, integrally, to my own society as, I believe, I belong, also integrally to some societies other than my own. The truth, of course, is that the modern African is no longer a product of an entirely indigenous culture. The modern sensibility which the modern poet is trying to express, is by its very nature complex, and it is a complex of values, some of which are indigenous, some of which are exotic, some of which are traditional, some of which are modern. Some of these values we are talking about are Christian, some are non-Christian, and I think that anybody who thinks it is possible to express consistently only one line of values, indigenous or exotic, is probably being artificial.[6]

Such an attitude is rare, even now, when so many African writers, obliged to pretend outrage over the supposed crimes of the colonial power, only succeed in limiting themselves. They refuse to see how much they belong in the European world as much they belong in the African, given that the literature they are in the process of creating is written, after all, in a European language. Okigbo understood the debt he owed to the tradition of English-language poetry, and he was fully prepared to exploit that tradition to make sense of his world. He could hardly do otherwise. Without a tradition of English-language African poetry against which he could work he needed to expropriate the only tradition that was available to him.

This is not to say that Okigbo did not feel the need to rescue his past from the dead hand of the British educational system which had done its best to convince him that his past something of which he ought to be ashamed. In this he shared the concerns of all but a few of the pioneers of modern Nigerian literature, most of whose early work was an attempt, as Achebe put it, to demonstrate 'that African people did not hear of culture for the first time from Europeans; that their societies were not mindless but frequently had a philosophy of great depth and beauty, that they had poetry and, above all, they had dignity'.[7] The sequence 'Heavensgate' is concerned with just this, where the protagonist returns to his village as a 'prodigal' in order to rediscover the world he had been taught to despise. It is what is fashionably known now as returning to his 'roots', and so it is. But he doesn't thereby repudiate his Catholicism, even after he gives vent to his anger over the violence Christianity perpetrated on African religions:

> Their talons they drew out of their scabbard,
> Upon the tree trunks, as if on fire-clay,
> Their beaks they sharpened;
> And spread like eagles their felt-wings,
> And descended upon the twin gods of Irkalla.

Okigbo is too generous, and too honest, to pretend that he can find sanctuary in traditional beliefs and obliterate the process that had made him the person he was. His concern was to find a way he could reconcile the two, being a product of both. In the earlier interview already referred to, he had this to say:

> I do not feel that as a Christian I have ever been uprooted from my own village gods. We have a goddess and a god in our family, our ancestral gods. And although I do not worship these actively, in the sense of offering them periodic sacrifices, I still feel that they are the people protecting me.
>
> But the way in which I think Christianity can be reconciled with this aspect of paganism is that I believe in fact all these gods are the same as the Christian God – that they are different aspects of the same power, the same force.[8]

That religion was important to Okigbo is evident in his poetry, where religious imagery is used extensively even when he is not directly concerned with religious experience. The very act of writing poetry, in fact, was profoundly religious, as he makes clear in the same interview: 'The way that I worship my gods is in fact through poetry. And I think that each poem I write is a ceremony of innocence, if you like. The creative process is a process of cleansing.'[9] This accounts both for the incantatory 'feel' to his verse, and the sometimes overpowering influence of T. S. Eliot, notably in the earlier poems. The influence gradually wanes until we come to the final sequence, 'Path of Thunder: Poems Prophesying War'. This sequence marks the transition from the personal themes of self-discovery to the public issues that were engulfing the country, a move that was begun in the two long poems which make up the sequence 'Silences'. It was a move from the self to the world, and a mark of his growing maturity as a poet.

Adewale Maja-Pearce

1 Marjory Whitelaw: 'Interview with Christopher Okigbo, 1967', *Journal of Commonwealth Literature*, No. 9, July 1970, p. 35.
2 In a private interview with the writer.
3 Sunday O. Anozie: *Christopher Okigbo*, Evans, London and Ibadan, 1972.
4 Chinua Achebe and Dubem Okafor (eds): *Don't Let Him Die*, Fourth Dimension, Enugu, 1978.
5 Ibid., p. vii.
6 'Interview with Okigbo' in Dennis Duerden and Cosmo Pieterse: *African Writers Talking*, Heinemann, London, 1972, p. 144.
7 Chinua Achebe: 'The Role of a Writer in a New Nation' in G.D. Killam (ed.): *African Writers on African Writing*, Heinemann, London, 1973, p. 8.
8 Marjory Whitelaw, op. cit., p. 30.
9 Ibid., p. 31.

I would like to thank the poet Steve Short for his help with this Introduction.

OKIGBO'S INTRODUCTION TO LABYRINTHS

◊

ALTHOUGH THESE poems were written and published separately, they are, in fact, organically related. *Heavensgate* was originally conceived as an Easter sequence. It later grew into a ceremony of innocence, something like a mass, an offering to Idoto, the village stream of which I drank, in which I washed, as a child; the celebrant, a personage like Orpheus, is about to begin a journey. Cleansing involves total nakedness, a complete self-surrender to the water spirit that nurtures all creation. The various sections of the poem, therefore, present this celebrant at various stations of his cross.

Limits and *Distances* are man's outer and inner worlds projected – the phenomenal and the imaginative, not in terms of their separateness but of their relationship – an attempt to reconcile the universal opposites of life and death in a live-die proposition: one is the other and either is both.

'Siren Limits' presents a protagonist in pursuit of the white elephant. In his progression to a sacred waterfront he falls victim to his own demonic obsession, becomes disembodied or loses his second self. 'Fragments out of the deluge' renders in retrospect certain details of the protagonist and of his milieu – the collective rape of innocence and profanation of the mysteries, in atonement for which he has had to suffer immolation. (*Limits* was written at the end of a journey of several centuries from Nsukka to Yola in pursuit of what turned out to be an illusion.)

Distances is, on the other hand, a poem of homecoming, but of homecoming in its spiritual and psychic aspect. The quest broken off after 'Siren Limits' is resumed, this time in the unconscious. The self that suffers, that experiences, ultimately finds fulfilment in a form of psychic union with the supreme spirit that is both destructive and creative. The process is one of sensual anaesthesia, of total liberation from all physical and emotional tension; the end result, a state of aesthetic grace. (*Distances* was written after my first experience of surgery under general anaesthesia.)

Between *Limits* and *Distances* an interval, *Silences*, is provided, in which two groups of mourners explore the possibilities of poetic metaphor in an attempt to elicit the music to which all imperishable cries must aspire. Both parts of *Silences* were inspired by the events of the day: *Lament of the Silent Sisters,* by the Western Nigeria Crisis of 1962, and the death of Patrice Lumumba; *Lament of the Drums*, by the imprisonment of Obafemi Awolowo, and the tragic death of his eldest son.

The 'Silent Sisters' are, however, sometimes like the drowning Franciscan nuns of Hopkins' *The Wreck of the Deutschland,* sometimes like the 'Sirenes' of

Debussy's *Nocturne* – two dissonant dreams associated in the dominant motif 'NO in thunder' (from one of Melville's letters to Hawthorne). This motif is developed by a series of related airs from sources as diverse as Malcolm Cowley, Raja Ratnam, Stephane Mallarmé, Rabindranath Tagore, Garçia Lorca and the yet unpublished Peter Thomas – airs which enable the 'Silent Sisters' to evoke, quite often by calling wolf, consonant tunes in life and letters. Section I, for instance, erects an illusion, a storm-tossed ship at mid-sea. The image of drowning virgins, and the dream of ultimate martyrdom are, however, also present. The illusion is enlarged by the motif of carrion-comfort (from one of Hopkins' poems). Section II develops this latter motif in the image of flies and splintered flames gloating over a carrion. The chorus breaks into a 'swan song' in Section III; and in the alternation (Section IV) between the Crier and the Chorus the sea herself, hidden face of the dream, is celebrated in her many colours. In Section V the main actors in the events of the day become almost recognizable in the opening couplets. The problem 'How does one say NO in thunder' is then finally resolved in silence. For the ultimate answer is to be sought only in terms of each poet's response to his medium.

The long-drums are, on the other hand, the spirits of the ancestors, the dead. They begin their lament by invoking the elements which make them up, and imploring evil forces to stay away from the rostrum. In Section II, the drums enter their theme song. They are coming out of their place of confinement, 'soot chamber', 'cinerary tower' (1st strophe), not to rejoice but to lament (2nd strophe). They are like urgent telegrams which are dispatched only when tragic events happen (3rd strophe). 'Babylonian capture', 'martyrdom' and 'chaliced vintage' suggest that someone might have been betrayed by his disciples (5th strophe). The alternation (in Section III) between the horns of elephant tusks (the italicised passages) and the drums establishes an identity between the personage of Section II, and Palinurus, the helmsman of Aeneas' ship during his legendary voyage to Italy. In Section IV, the drums return to their theme song, weary and exhausted from the long excursion of Section III. After a few limbering-up passages (1st, 2nd and 3rd strophes) a treble drum takes a six-phrase solo (4th strophe) A six-phrase response by the mother-of-drums (5th strophe) leads on to the re-entry of the horns in a variation on Ishthar's lament for Tammuz (Section V). Here the theme of the poem is no longer suggested but stated; the personages of the earlier sections together become fused with that of Tammuz, and consequently with the movement of the seasons.

Labyrinths is thus a fable of man's perennial quest for fulfilment. (The title may suggest Minos' legendary palace at Cnossus, but the double headed axe is as much a symbol of sovereignty in traditional Ibo society as in Crete. Besides, the long and tortuous passage to the shrine of the 'long-juju' of the Aro Ibos may perhaps, best be described as a labyrinth.) Inevitably, several presences haunt the complex of rooms and ante-rooms, of halls and corridors that lead to the palace of the White Goddess, and in which a country visitor might easily lose his way. Nevertheless, a poet-protagonist is assumed throughout; a personage, however, much larger than Orpheus; one with a load of destiny on his head, rather like Gilgamesh, like Aeneas, like the hero of Melville's *Moby Dick,* like the Fisher King of Eliot's *Waste Land*; a personage for whom the progression through 'Heavensgate' through 'Limits' through 'Distances' is like telling the beads of a rosary; except that the beads are neither stone nor agate but globules of anguish strung together on memory.

Every work of this kind is necessarily a cry of anguish – of the root extending its branches of coral, of corals extending their roots into each living hour; the swell of the silent sea the great heaving dream at its highest, the thunder of splitting pods – the tears scatter, take root, the cotyledons broken, burgeon into laughter of leaf; or else rot into vital hidden roles in the nitrogen cycle. The present dream clamoured to be born a cadenced cry: silence to appease the fever of flight beyond the iron gate.

Ibadan
October 1965

ACKNOWLEDGEMENTS FOR
LABYRINTHS

◊

FOR PERMISSION to reprint I am grateful to the editor of
Transition in which the earliest versions of 'Limits',
'Silences' and 'Distances' made their first public
appearance; and to Mbari Publications under whose
imprint *Heavensgate* (1962), *Limits* (1964) and *Silences*
(1965) have previously been published. The versions
here preserved are, however, somewhat different and
are final.

I am also grateful to novelists Chinua Achebe and
Dennis Williams, critics Ulli Beier and Gerald Moore,
for constant interest and encouragement; to critic Sunday Anozie, and poet Paul Theroux, who share with
me the experience of *Labyrinths*; and to Benedict
Obumselu for criticisms that continue to guide me
along the paths of greater clarity.

PART ONE:
EARLY POEMS

◊

ON THE NEW YEAR

LOVE APART

MOONGLOW

FOUR CANZONES

ON THE NEW YEAR

Now it is over, the midnight funeral that parts
The old year from the new;
And now beneath each pew
The warden dives to find forgotten missals
Scraps of resolutions and medals;
And over lost souls in the graves
Amid the tangled leaves
The Wagtail is singing:
Cheep cheep cheep the new year is coming;
Christ will come again, the churchbell is tinging
Christ will come again after the argument in heaven
Christ . . . Nichodemus . . . Magdalen . . .
Ding dong ding . . . . . .

And the age rolls on like a wind glassed flood,
And the pilgrimage to the cross is the void . . .

And into time time slips with a lazy pace
And time into time
And need we wait while time and the hour
Roll, waiting for power?

II

To wait is to linger
With the hope that the flood will flow dry;
To hope is to point an expectant finger
At fate, fate that has long left us to lie
Marooned on the sands
Left with dry glands
To suckle as die.

Wait indeed, wait with grief laden
Hearts that throb like a diesel engine.
Throbbing with hopes:
Those hopes of men those hopes that are nowhere,
Those nebulous hopes, sand castles in the air —

Wait and hope?
The way is weary and long and time is
Fast on our heels;
Or forces life to a headlong conclusion
Nor yet like crafty Heracles
Devolve on someone else
The bulk of the globe?

III

Where then are the roots, where the solution
To life's equation?

The roots are nowhere
There are no roots here
Probe if you may
From now until doomsday.

We have to think of ourselves as forever
Soaring and sinking like dead leaves blown by a gust
Floating choicelessly to the place where
Old desires and new born hopes like bubbles burst
Into nothing – blown to the place of fear
To the cross in the void;
Or else forever playing this zero-sum game
With fate as mate, and forever
Slaying and mating as one by one
Our tombstones rise in the void.

(*1958*)

LOVE APART

The moon has ascended between us
Between two pines
That bow to each other

Love with the moon has ascended
Has fed on our solitary pines

And we are now shadows
That cling to each other
But kiss the air only.

(1960)

MOONGLOW

Moonglow . . .
after the travail in gloom
moonglow . . .
naked in her bloom:

And there engraved on the dead world,
Moonman,
bowed in shame over the beam
I see you,
hear ever your penance as you measure
   cup after cup your strength,
and Time,
   day after day its length.

(Ibadan, 1960)

7

FOUR CANZONES: 1957–1961

1 SONG OF THE FOREST

(with Urbo)

You loaf, child of the forest,
beneath a village umbrella,
plucking from tender string a
    Song of the forest.
Me, away from home, run-
away, must leave the borders of our
land, fruitful fields,
    must leave our homeland.

But you, child of the forest,
loaf beneath an umbrella,
teaching the woods to sing a
    song of the forest.

(Lagos, 1958; based on Virgil's Tityrus*)*

2 DEBTORS' LANE

(with drums and ogene)

A & B: THIS is debtors' lane, this is
    the new haven, where wrinkled faces
    watch the wall clock strike each hour
    in a dry cellar.

A: No heavenly transports now
of youthful passion
and the endless succession
of tempers and moods
in high societies;
no blasts no buffets
of a mad generation
nor the sonorous arguments
of the hollow brass
and the copious cups
of fraudulent misses
in brothels
of a mad generation.

A & B: HERE rather let us lie in a new haven,
drinking in the air that we breathe in
until it chokes us and we die.
Here rather let us lie with wrinkled faces
watching the wall clock strike each hour
in a dry cellar.

B: There was the tenement
in hangman's lane
where repose was a dream
unreal
and a knock on the door
at dawn
hushed the tenant humped
beneath the bed:
was it the postman
or the bailiff with a writ?
And if the telephone rang
alas, if the telephone rang . . .
Was he to hang up his life
on a rock
and answer the final call?

9

A & B: HERE rather let us rest in a new haven
awaiting the tap tap tap on the door
that brings in light at dawn.
Here rather let us rest with wrinkled faces
watching the wall clock strike each hour
in a dry cellar.

(Fiditi, 1959)

3 LAMENT OF THE FLUTES

(with two flutes)

TIDEWASH . . . Memories
fold-over-fold free-furrow,
mingling old tunes with new.
Tidewash . . . Ride me
memories, astride on firm
saddle, wreathed with white
lilies & roses of blood . . .

Sing to the rustic flute:
Sing a new note . . .

Where are the Maytime flowers,
where the roses? What will the
Watermaid bring at sundown,
a garland? A handful of tears?
Sing to the rustic flute:
Sing a new note . . .

Comes Dawn
gasping thro worn lungs,
Day breathes,
panting like torn horse —

We follow the wind to the fields
Bruising grass leafblade and corn . . .

Sundown: I draw in my egg head.
Night falls
smearing sore bruises with *Sloan*'s
boring new holes in old sheets –

We hear them, the talkative pines,
And nightbirds and woodnymphs afar off . . .

Shall I answer their call,
creep on my underself
out of my snug hole, out of my shell
to the rocks and the fringe for cleansing?
Shall I offer to *Idoto*
my sandhouse and bones,
then write no more on snow-patch?

Sing to the rustic flute.
Sing a new note.

(Ojoto, 1960)

4 L A M E N T O F T H E
L A V E N D E R M I S T

(with three flutes)

(i)

BLACK dolls
Returning from the foam:
Two faces of a coin
That meet afar off . . .

11

Sea smiles at a distance
   with lips of foam
Sea walks like a rainbow
   beyond them.

And voice
Returning from a dream,
Descends, rejoices –
Air, sun, blood . . .
   And wakes us . . .
DOLLS . . .
Forms
Of memory
To be worshipped
Adored
By innocence:

Creatures of the mind's eye
Barren –
Of memory –
Remembrance of things past.

Eagles in space and earth and sky
Shadows of sin in grove of orange,
Of altar-penitence
Over me at sundown,
Of wind on leaves,
A song of Christmas of –
Echoes in the prison of the mind.
Shadows of song of love's stillness,
Shadows of the stillness of the song
   Over me at sundown
   In an empty garden
     Where
Wounded by the wind lie dead leaves.

AT THE FIRST fork of the road
Saint Vitus's dancer,
At the fork of the lightening
Lady of the lavender –
   mist, scattering
Lightening shafts without rain,
   came forging
Thunder with no smell of water –

   Abyss of wonders,
Of masks, black masks, idols,
From whose nest of fireflies,
   Phosphorescence
   Over me at sundown
   In an empty garden
Wounded by the wind lie dead leaves.

(iii)

TAKE HER to an island in the sun,
Wrap her round your loin and run,
Stolen from her prison.
TAKE HER to a mountain waterfall,
Strike her with the wind beneath starfall,
Stolen from her prison.

(iv)

AND SHE took me to the river
Believing me a child –
   Spirit of the wind and the waves –
offering me love in a
Feeding bottle –
   Kernels of the water of the sky –
And she led me by the water
Believing me a child –
   Echoes of the waters of the beginning –
But the outstretched love
Dried as it reached me –
   Shadows of the fires of the end.
   The moon has ascended between us –
   Between two pines
   That bow to each other;
   Love with the moon has ascended,
   Has fed on our solitary stems;
   And we are now shadows
   That cling to each other
   But kiss the air only.

(Nsukka, 1961)

14

PART TWO:
LABYRINTHS

◊

HEAVENSGATE

LIMITS

SILENCES

DISTANCES

HEAVENSGATE

I THE PASSAGE

BEFORE YOU, mother Idoto,[1]
  naked I stand;
before your watery presence,
  a prodigal

leaning on an oilbean,
lost in your legend.

Under your power wait I
  on barefoot,
watchman for the watchword
  at *Heavensgate;*

out of the depths my cry:
give ear and hearken . . .

---

[1] A village stream. The oilbean, the tortoise and the python are totems for her worship.

DARK WATERS of the beginning.

Rays, violet and short, piercing the gloom,
foreshadow the fire that is dreamed of.

Rainbow on far side, arched like a boa bent to kill,
foreshadows the rain that is dreamed of.

Me to the orangery
solitude invites,
a wagtail, to tell
the tangled-wood-tale;
a sunbird, to mourn
a mother on a spray.

Rain and sun in single combat;
on one leg standing,
in silence at the passage,
the young bird at the passage.

SILENT FACES at crossroads:
    festivity in black . . .

Faces of black like long black
    column of ants,

behind the bell tower,
into the hot garden
where all roads meet:
festivity in black . . .

O Anna at the knobs of the panel oblong,
hear us at crossroads at the great hinges

where the players of loft pipe organs
rehearse old lovely fragments, alone –

strains of pressed orange leaves on pages,
bleach of the light of years held in leather:

For we are listening in cornfields
    among the windplayers,
listening to the wind leaning over
    its loveliest fragment . . .

II INITIATIONS

SCAR OF the crucifix
over the breast,
by red blade inflicted
by red-hot blade,
on right breast witnesseth

mystery which I, initiate,
received newly naked
upon waters of the genesis
from Kepkanly.[1]

Elemental, united in vision
of present and future,
the pure line, whose innocence
denies inhibitions.

At confluence of planes, the angle:
man loses man, loses vision;

so comes John the Baptist
with bowl of salt water
preaching the gambit:
life without sin, without

life; which accepted,
way leads downward
down orthocenter
avoiding decisions.

[1] A half-serious half-comical primary school teacher of the late thirties.

Or forms fourth angle –
duty, obligation:

square yields the moron,
fanatics and priests and popes,
organizing secretaries and
party managers; better still,

the rhombus – brothers and deacons,
liberal politicians,
selfish selfseekers – all who are good
doing nothing at all;

the quadrangle, the rest, me and you . . .

Mystery, which barring
the errors of the rendering
witnesseth
red-hot blade on right breast
the scar of the crucifix.

and the hand fell with Haragin,[1]
Kepkanly that wielded the blade;

with Haragin with God's light between them:

but the solitude within me remembers Kepkanly . . .

[1] Kepkanly was reported to have died from excess of joy when he
received arrears of salary awarded by the Haragin Commission of 1945.

AND THIS from Jadum,[1]

(Say if thou knowest
from smell of the incense
a village where liveth
in heart of the grassland
a minstrel who singeth)

to shepherds, with a lute on his lip:

Do not wander in speargrass,
After the lights,
Probing lairs in stockings,
To roast
The viper alive, with dog lying
Upsidedown in the crooked passage . . .

Do not listen at keyholes,
After the lights,
To smell from other rooms,
After the lights –

Singeth Jadum from Rockland,
after the lights.

And there are here
the errors of the rendering . . .

[1] A half-demented village minstrel

AND THIS from Upandru:[1]

Screen your bedchamber thoughts
with sun-glasses,
who could jump your eye,
your mind-window,

And I said:
The prophet only the poet.
And he said: Logistics.
(Which is what poetry is) . . .

And he said to the ram: Disarm.
And I said:
Except by rooting,
who could pluck yam tubers from their base?

And there are here
the errors of the rendering . . .

[1] A village explainer

25

III WATERMAID

EYE OPEN on the sea,
eyes open, of the prodigal;
upward to heaven shoot
where stars will fall from.

Secret I have told into no ear,
save into a dughole, to hold, not to drown with –
Secret I have planted into beachsand

now breaks
salt-white surf on the stones and me,
and lobsters and shells
in iodine smell –
maid of the salt-emptiness,
sophisticreamy,

whose secret I have covered up with beachsand . . .

Shadow of rain over sunbeaten beach,
shadow of rain over man with woman.

BRIGHT
with the armpit-dazzle of a lioness,
she answers,

wearing white light about her;

and the waves escort her,
my lioness,
crowned with moonlight.

So brief her presence –
match-flare in wind's breath –
so brief with mirrors around me.

Downward . . .
the waves distil her;
gold crop
sinking ungathered.

Watermaid of the salt-emptiness,
grown are the ears of the secret.

AND I WHO am here abandoned,

count the sand by wavelash abandoned,
count her blessing, my white queen.

But the spent sea reflects
from his mirrored visage
not my queen, a broken shadow.

So I who count in my island the moments,
count the hour which will bring

my lost queen with angels' ash in the wind.

THE STARS have departed,
the sky in monocle
surveys the worldunder.

The stars have departed,
and I – where am I?

Stretch, stretch, O antennae,
to clutch at this hour,

fulfilling each moment in a
broken monody.

SO WOULD I to the hills again
so would I
to where springs the fountain
there to draw from

And to hill top clamber
body and soul
whitewashed in the moondew
there to see from

So would I from my eye the mist
so would I
thro' moonmist to hilltop
there for the cleansing

Here is a new laid egg
here a white hen at midterm.

THE FLOWER weeps, unbruised,
for him who was silenced
whose advent dumb-bells celebrate
in dim light with wine song:

Messiah will come again
After the argument in heaven
Messiah will come again . . .

Fingers of penitence bring
to a palm grove
vegetable offering with five
fingers of chalk . . .

THUNDERING drums and cannons
in palm grove:
the spirit is in ascent.

I have visited;
on palm beam imprinted
my pentagon –

I have visited, the prodigal . . .

In palm grove,
long-drums and cannons:
the spirit in the ascent.

V   NEWCOMER

TIME for worship –

softly sing the bells of exile,
the angelus,
softly sings my guardian angel.

Mask over my face –

my own mask, not ancestral – I sign:
remembrance of calvary,
and of age of innocence, which is of . . .

Time for worship:

Anna of the panel oblongs,
    protect me
from them fucking angels;
    protect me
my sandhouse and bones.

For Georgette

IN THE CHILL breath of the day's waking,
comes the newcomer,

when the draper of May
has sold out fine green garments,

and the hillsides have made up their faces,
and the gardens, on their faces a painted smile:

such synthetic welcome at the cock's third siren;
when from behind the bulrushes

waking, in the teeth of the chill May morn,
comes the newcomer.

I AM standing above the noontide,
Above the bridgehead;

Listening to the laughter of waters
    that do not know why:

Listening to incense –

I am standing above the noontide
    with my head above it;

Under my feet float the waters
Tide blows them under . . .

LIMITS

SUDDENLY becoming talkative
  like weaverbird
Summoned at offside of
  dream remembered

Between sleep and waking,
I hang up my egg-shells
To you of palm grove,
Upon whose bamboo towers

Hang, dripping with yesterupwine,
A tiger mask and nude spear . . .

Queen of the damp half light,
I have had my cleansing,
Emigrant with air-borne nose,
The he-goat-on-heat.

II

FOR HE WAS a shrub among the poplars,
Needing more roots
More sap to grow to sunlight,
Thirsting for sunlight,

A low growth among the forest.

Into the soul
The selves extended their branches,
Into the moments of each living hour,
Feeling for audience

Straining thin among the echoes;

And out of the solitude
Voice and soul with selves unite,
Riding the echoes,

Horsemen of the apocalypse;

And crowned with one self
The name displays its foliage,
Hanging low

A green cloud above the forest.

III

BANKS of reed.
Mountains of broken bottles.

& the mortar is not yet dry . . .

Silent the footfall,
Soft as cat's paw,
Sandalled in velvet in fur,

So we must go, eve-mist on shoulders,
Sun's dust of combat,
With brand burning out at hand-end.

& the mortar is not yet dry . . .

Then we must sing, tongue-tied,
Without name or audience,
Making harmony among the branches.

And this is the crisis point,
The twilight moment between
    sleep and waking;
And voice that is reborn transpires,
Not thro' pores in the flesh,
    but the soul's back-bone.

Hurry on down –
    Thro' the high-arched gate –
Hurry on down
    little stream to the lake;

Hurry on down –
    Thro' the cinder market –
Hurry on down
    in the wake of the dream;

Hurry on down –
    To rockpoint of Cable,[1]

To pull by the rope
    the big white elephant . . .

& the mortar is not yet dry
& the mortar is not yet dry;

And the dream wakes
    the voice fades
In the damp half light
    like a shadow,

Not leaving a mark.

[1] Cable Point at Asaba, a sacred waterfront with rocky promontory, and terminal point of a traditional quinquennial pilgrimage.

IV

AN IMAGE insists
From flag pole of the heart;
Her image distracts
With the cruelty of the rose . . .

Oblong-headed lioness –
No shield is proof against her –
Wound me, O sea-weed
Face, blinded like strong-room –

Distances of her armpit-fragrance
Turn chloroform enough for my patience –

When you have finished
& done up my stitches,
Wake me near the altar,
& this poem will be finished . . .

V – XII FRAGMENTS OUT OF THE DELUGE

ON AN empty sarcophagus
    hewn out of alabaster,
A branch of fennel on an
    empty sarcophagus[1] . . .

Nothing suggests accident
    where the beast[2]
Is finishing her rest . . .

Smoke of ultramarine and amber
Floats above the fields after
Moonlit rains, from tree unto tree
Distils the radiance of a king[3] . . .

You might as well see the new branch of Enkidu;[4]
And that is no new thing either . . .

---

[1] The body of one of the Egyptian Pharaohs is said to have meta-morphosed into a fennel branch.

[2] The lioness of LIMITS IV who destroyed the hero's second self.

[3] The hero is like Gilgamesh, legendary king of Uruk in Mesopotamia, and first human hero in literature.

[4] Companion and second self of Gilgamesh.

VI

HE STOOD in the midst of them all
   and appeared in true form,
He found them drunken, he found none
   thirsty among them.

Who would add to your statue,
Or in your village accept you?

He fed them on seed wrapped in wonders;
They deemed it a truth-value system,
   Man out of innocence,
And there was none thirsty among them.

They cast him in mould of iron,
And asked him to do a rock-drill –
   Man out of innocence –
He drilled with dumb-bells about him.

And they took the key off
And they hid the key of . . .
That none may enter.

And they took the hot spoils off the battle,
And they shared the hot spoils among them:

Estates, among them;
And they were the chosen,
   mongrel breeds,
With slogan in hand, of
   won divination . . .

And you talk of the people:
There is none thirsty among them.

45

VII

AND FROM frame of iron,
And in mould of iron . . .

For he ate the dead lion,
& was within the corpse –

Which is not the point;
And who says it matters
Which way the kite flows,
Provided the movement is
Around the burning market –

  And lilies
Sprouted from rosebeds,
  Canalilies,
Like tombstones from pavements;

And to the cross in the void came pilgrims;
Came, floating with burnt-out tapers;

Past the village orchard where
Flannagan[1]
Preached the Pope's message,
To where drowning nuns suspired,
Asking the key-word from stone;
& he said:

To sow the fireseed among grasses,
& lo, to keep it till it burns out . . .

[1] A well-known Irish priest of the 1940s.

VIII

BUT THE sunbird repeats
Over the oilbean shadows:

'A fleet of eagles,
    over the oilbean shadows,
Holds the square
    under curse of their breath.

Beaks of bronze, wings
    of hard-tanned felt,
The eagles flow
    over man-mountains,
Steep walls of voices,
    horizons;
The eagles furrow
    dazzling over the voices
With wings like
    combs in the wind's hair

Out of the solitude, the fleet,
Out of the solitude,
Intangible like silk thread of sunlight,
The eagles ride low,
Resplendent . . . resplendent;
And small birds sing in shadows,
Wobbling under their bones . . .'

IX

AND, squatting,
A blind dog[1] howls at his godmother:

Eunice[2] at the passageway,
Singing the moon to sleep over the hills,
Eunice at the passageway . . .

Give him no chair, they say,
The dawn's charioteer,
Riding with the angry stars
Toward the great sunshine.

[1] Known for his power of prophecy.
[2] My childhood nurse known for her lyricism.

48

X

AND TO US they came –
Malisons, malisons, mair than ten –
And climbed the bombax
And killed the Sunbird.

And they scanned the forest of oilbean,
Its approach; surveyed its high branches . . .

And they entered into the forest,
And they passed through the forest of oilbean
And found them, the twin-gods[1] of the forest . . .

And the beasts broke –
Malisons, malisons, mair than ten –
And dawn-gust grumbled,
Fanning the grove
Like a horse-tail-man,
Like handmaid of dancers,
Fanning their branches.

Their talons they drew out of their scabbard,
Upon the tree trunks, as if on fire-clay,
Their beaks they sharpened;
And spread like eagles their felt-wings,
And descended upon the twin gods of Irkalla[2]

And the ornaments of him,
And the beads about his tail;
And the carapace of her,
And her shell, they divided.

[1] The tortoise and the python.
[2] In Sumerian myth, queen of the underworld.

49

XI

AND THE gods lie in state
And the gods lie in state
Without the long-drum.

And the gods lie unsung,
Veiled only with mould,
Behind the shrinehouse.

Gods grow out,
Abandoned;
And so do they . . .

XII

BUT AT THE window, outside, a shadow:

The sunbird sings again
From the LIMITS of the dream;
The Sunbird sings again
Where the caress does not reach,

   of Guernica,[1]
On whose canvas of blood,
The slits of his tongue
   cling to glue . . .

& the cancelling out is complete.

[1] A work by Picasso.

SILENCES

LAMENT OF THE
SILENT SISTERS

LAMENT OF THE DRUMS

LAMENT OF THE
SILENT SISTERS

I

Crier: IS THERE . . . Is certainly there . . .
For as in sea-fever globules of fresh anguish
immense golden eggs empty of albumen
sink into our balcony . . .

How does one say NO in thunder . . .

For in breakers in sea-fever compass or cross
makes a difference: certainly makes
not an escape ladder . . .

Where is there for us an anchorage;
A shank for a sheet, a double arch –

Chorus: They comb the afternoon the scavengers
For scented shadows above the underrush –

Crier: The cross to us we still call to us,
In this jubilee-dance above the carrion . . .

II

Chorus: THIS SHADOW of carrion incites
  and in rhythms of silence
Urges us; gathers up our broken
  hidden feather-of-flight,
To this anguished cry of Moloch:

What cast-iron steps cascading down the valley
  all forged into thunder of tanks;
And detonators cannoned into splintered flames,
  in this jubilee-dance of fireflies!

Crier: They struck him in the ear they struck him in the eye;
They picked his bones for scavenging:

Chorus: And there will be a continual going to the well,
Until they smash their calabashes.

Crier: So, one dips one's tongue in ocean, and begins
To cry to the mushroom of the sky:

III

Chorus: DUMB-BELLS outside the gates
In hollow seascapes without memory, we carry
Each of us an urn of native
Earth, a double handful anciently gathered.

And by salt mouths by yellow
Sand banks sprinkled with memories, we spread
To the nightairs our silences,
Suffused in this fragrance of divers melodies:

Crier: This is our swan song
This is our senses' stillness:

Chorus: We carry in our worlds that flourish
Our worlds that have failed . . .

Crier: This is our swan song
This is the sigh of our spirits:

Chorus: Unseen shadows like long-fingered winds
Pluck from our strings
This shriek, the music of the firmament . . .

IV

Alternatively
Crier: *Chorus:* I SEE many colours in the salt teeth of foam

　　　　　Which is no where to face under the half-light

　　　　　The rainbow they say is full of harmonies

　　　　　We shall make a grey turn to face it.

　　　　　Wild winds cry out against us

　　　　　We shall swallow our heart in our stomach

　　　　　More wrinkles on the salt face of glass

　　　　　The winds' broom sweeps only the surface.

　　　　　I hear many voices about us

　　　　　We shall wear the green habit of kolanuts

　　　　　The kingfisher gathers his ropes in the distance

　　　　　The sweet water gathers them inward

　　　　　The dipping paddle blades, the inconstant dolphins

　　　　　The salt water gathers them inward

　　　　　Will the water gather us in her sibylline chamber?

　　　　　And our silences fade into galloping antelopes?

V

Alternatively
Crier: *Chorus:* YELLOW images:
           Voices in the senses' stillness . . .

           Pointed arches:
           Pieces in the form of a pear . . .

           Angles, filaments:
           Hosts of harlequins in the shadows:

           And bearded Judas,
           Resplendent among the dancers . . .

           I hear sounds as, they say,
           A worshipper hears the flutes –

           The music sounds so in the soul
           It can hear nothing else –

           I hear painted harmonies
           From the mushroom of the sky –

           Silences are melodies
           Heard in retrospect:

           And how does one say NO in thunder?

One dips one's tongue in the ocean;
Camps with the choir of inconstant
Dolphins, by shallow sand banks
Sprinkled with memories;
Extends one's branches of coral,
The branches extends in the senses'
Silence; this silence distills
in yellow melodies.

L A M E N T O F T H E D R U M S

I

LION-HEARTED cedar forest, gonads for our thunder,
Even if you are very far away, we invoke you:

Give us our hollow heads of long-drums . . .

Antelopes for the cedar forest, swifter messengers
Than flash-of-beacon-flame, we invoke you:

Hide us; deliver us from our nakedness . . .

Many-fingered canebrake, exile for our laughter,
Even if you are very far away, we invoke you:

Come; limber our raw hides of antelopes . . .

Thunder of tanks of giant iron steps of detonators,
Fail safe from the clearing, we implore you:

We are tuned for a feast-of-seven-souls . . .

II

AND THE DRUMS once more
From our soot chamber,
From the cinerary tower
To the crowded clearing;

Long-drums, we awake
Like a shriek of incense,
The unheard sullen shriek
Of the funerary ram:

Liquid messengers of blood,
Like urgent telegrams,
We have never been deployed
For feast of antelopes . . .

And to the Distant – but how shall we go?
The robbers will strip us of our tendons!

For we sense
With dog-nose a Babylonian capture,
The martyrdom
Blended into that chaliced vintage;

And savour
The incense and in high buskin,
Like a web
Of voices all rent by javelins.

But distant seven winds invite us and our cannons
To limber our membranes for a dance of elephants . . .

III

THEY ARE FISHING *today in the dark waters*
Where the mariner is finishing his rest . . .

Palinurus, alone in a hot prison, you will keep
The dead sea awake with nightsong . . .

Silver of rivulets this side of the bridge,
Cascades of lily-livered laughter,
Fold-on-fold of raped, naked blue —
What memory has the sea of her lover?

Palinurus, unloved in your empty catacomb,
You will wear away through age alone . . .

Nothing remains, only smoke after storm —
Some strange Celaeno and her harpy crew,
Laden with night and their belly's excrement,
Profane all things with hooked feet and foul teeth —

Masks and beggar-masks without age or shadow:
Broken tin-gods whose vision is dissolved . . .

It is over, Palinurus, at least for you,
In your tarmac of night and fever-dew:

Tears of grace, not of sorrow, broken
In two, protest your inviolable image;

And the sultry waters, touched by the sun,
Inherit your paleness who reign, resigned

Like palm oil fostered in an ancient clay bowl;
A half-forgotten name; like a stifled sneeze . . .

Fishermen out there in the dark – O you
Who rake the waves or chase their wake –
Weave for him a shadow out of your laughter
For a dumb child to hide his nakedness . . .

IV

AND THE DRUMS
Once more and like masked dancers,
On the orange –
Yellow myth of the sands of exile –

Long-drums dis-
Jointed, and with bleeding tendons,
Like tarantulas
Emptied of their bitterest poisons,

And to the Distant – but how shall we go?
The robbers will strip us of our thunder . . .

– So, like a dead letter unanswered,
   Our rococo
   Choir of insects is null
   Cacophony
   And void as a debt summons served
   On a bankrupt;

– But the antiphony, still clamorous,
   In tremolo,
   Like an afternoon, for shadows;
   And the winds
   The distant seven cannons invite us
   To a sonorous

Ishthar's lament for Tammuz:

V

FOR THE FAR *removed there is wailing:*

For the far removed;
For the Distant . . .

The wailing is for the fields of crop:

The drums' lament is:
They grow not . . .

The wailing is for the fields of men:

For the barren wedded ones;
For perishing children . . .

The wailing is for the Great River:

Her pot-bellied watchers
Despoil her . . .

DISTANCES

I

FROM FLESH into phantom on the horizontal stone
I was the sole witness to my homecoming . . .

Serene lights on the other balcony:
redolent fountains bristling with signs –

But what does my divine rejoicing hold?
A bowl of incense, a nest of fireflies?

I was the sole witness to my homecoming . . .

For in the inflorescence of the white
chamber, a voice, from very far away,
chanted, and the chamber descanted, the birthday of earth,
paddled me home through some dark
labyrinth, from laughter to the dream.

Miner into my solitude,
incarnate voice of the dream,
you will go,
with me as your chief acolyte,
again into the anti-hill . . .

I was the sole witness to my homecoming . . .

II

DEATH LAY in ambush that evening in that island;
voice sought its echo that evening in that island.

And the eye lost its light,
the light lost its shadow.

For the wind, eternal suitor of dead leaves,
unrolled his bandages to the finest swimmer . . .

It was an evening without flesh or skeleton;
an evening with no silver bells to its tale;
without lanterns, an evening without buntings;
and it was an evening without age or memory –

for we are talking of such commonplaces,
and on the brink of such great events . . .

And in the freezing tuberoses of the white
chamber, eyes that had lost their animal
colour, havoc of eyes of incandescent rays,
pinned me, cold, to the marble stretcher,

until my eyes lost their blood
and the blood lost its odour,

and the everlasting fire from the oblong window
forgot the taste of ash in the air's marrow:

anguish and solitude . . .
Smothered, my scattered
cry, the dancers,
lost among their own
snares; the faces,
the hands held captive;
the interspaces
reddening with blood;

and behind them all,
in smock of white cotton,
Death herself,
the chief celebrant,
in a cloud of incense,
paring her fingernails . . .

At her feet rolled their heads like cut fruits;
about her fell
their severed members, numerous as locusts.

Like split wood left to dry, the dismembered
joints of the ministrants piled high.

She bathed her knees in the blood of attendants;
her smock in entrails of ministrants . . .

III

IN THE scattered line of pilgrims
bound for Shibboleth
in my hand the crucifix
the torn branch the censer

In the scattered line of pilgrims
from Dan to Beersheeba
camphor iodine chloroform
either sting me in the bum

On the stone steps on the marble
beyond the balcony
prophets martyrs lunatics
like the long stride of the evening

At the clearing dantini
in the garden dillettanti;
vendors princes negritude
politicians in the tall wood . . .

IV

AND AT THE archway
a triangular lintel
of solid alabaster
enclosed in a square
inscribed in a circle
with a hollow centre,
above the archway
yawning shutterless
like celestial pincers
like a vast countenance:

the only way to go
through the marble archway
to the catatonic pingpong
of the evanescent halo . . .

And beyond the archway
like pentecostal orbs
resplendent far distant
in the intangible void
an immense crucifix
of phosphorescent mantles:

after we had formed
then only the forms were formed
and all the forms
were formed after our forming . . .

V

SWEAT OVER hoof in ascending gestures –
each step is the step of the mule in the abyss –
the archway the oval the panel oblong
to that sanctuary at the earth's molten bowel
for the music woven into the funerary rose
the water in the tunnel its effervescent laughter
the open laughter of the grape or vine
the question in the inkwell the answer on the monocle
the unanswerable question in the tabernacle's silence –

Censers, from the cradle,
of a nameless religion:

each sigh is time's stillness, in the abyss . . .

Mated and sealed
in a proud oblation,

brothers to silence and the wandering rocks;

with the burden of the pawn,
on the molten stone,

and the scar of the kiss and of the two swords.

Sweat over hoof
in the settled abyss:

each sigh is the stillness of the kiss . . .

VI

THE SEASON the season
the tall wood the clearing
the season the season
the stone steps the dream . . .

Come into my cavern,
Shake the mildew from your hair;
Let your ear listen:
My mouth calls from a cavern . . .

Lo, it is the same blood that flows . . .

Shadows distances labyrinths violences,
Skeletal oblong
of my sentient being, I receive you
in my perforated
mouth of a stranger: empty of meaning,
stones without juice –

the goat still knows its fodder,
the leopards on its trail –

For it is the same blood,
through the same orifices,
the same branches
trembling intertwined,
and the same faces
in the interspaces.

And it is the same breath, liquid, without acolyte,
like invisible mushrooms on stone surfaces.

And at this chaste instant of delineated anguish,
the same voice, importunate, aglow with the goddess –

unquenchable, yellow, darkening homeward
like a cry of wolf above crumbling houses –

strips the dream naked,
bares the entrails;

and in the orangery of immense corridors,
I wash my feet in your pure head, O maid,

and walk along your feverish, solitary shores,

seeking, among your variegated teeth,
the tuberose of my putrescent laughter:

I have fed out of the drum
I have drunk out of the cymbal

I have entered your bridal
chamber; and lo,

I am the sole witness to my homecoming.

PART THREE:
LATE POEMS

◊

LAMENT OF THE MASKS

DANCE OF THE
PAINTED MAIDENS

PATH OF THUNDER:
POEMS PROPHESYING WAR

LAMENT
OF THE MASKS

(For W.B. Yeats)

For the time has come O Poet,
To descant your praise-names . . .

I

AT THE BEND of the road,
The last bend before the broken teeth of the river:

And the rumour awakens
Like smell of wet earth after rain,
Elephant-feathered breed,

Burgeons into clamour, mounts up, caparisoned,
Charges to the assault;

And in cold and blue
Of iron-mask, envelopes the haven in which
Catechumen rehearse,

Like snails on anthills, whispered canticles:

Warped voices –
For we answer the cannon
From far off –

And from throats of iron –

In bird-masks –
Unlike accusing tones that issue forth javelins –
Bring, O Poet,

Panegyrics for the arch-priest of the sanctuary . . .

II

WAGGONER of the great Dawn –
For it is forbidden to mention your name –

How many beacon flames
Can ever challenge the sun?

Water of baptism,
Ladder to the ethereal ivory tower –

Ten thousand rivers
Can never challenge the sea.

Thunder above the earth,
Sacrifice too huge for the vulture –

Twenty thousand cannons
Must still do homage to your breath.

Hunter of elephants,
Earth tremor upon the land –

For the time has come, O Poet,
To descant your praise-names –

III

THEY THOUGHT you would stop pursuing the
   white elephant
They thought you would stop pursuing the white
   elephant
But you pursued the white elephant without turning
   back –
You who chained the white elephant with your
   magic flute
You who trapped the white elephant like a common
   rabbit
You who sent the white elephant trembling into
   your net –
And stripped him of his horns, and made them
   your own
You who fashioned his horns into ivory trumpets –

They put you into the eaves thatch
You split the thatch
They poured you into an iron mould
You burst the mould;

For like the dog's mouth you were never at rest,
Who, fighting a battle in front,
Mapped out, with dust-of-combat ahead of you,
The next battle field at the rear –

That generations unborn
Might never taste the steel –

Who converted a jungle into marble palaces
Who watered a dry valley and weeded its banks –

For we had almost forgotten
Your praise-names –

Who transformed a desert into green pasture
Who commanded highways to pass thro the forest –
And will remain a mountain
Even in your sleep . . .

IV

BUT WILL a flutist never stop to wipe his nose?
Two arms can never encircle a giant iroko.

Night breezes drum on the plantain leaf:
Let the plantain leaf take over the dance . . .

(*I am indebted to Mr Ben Obumselu of Ibadan University English
Department for criticisms which led to improvements in phrase and
structure –* Christopher Okigbo.)

DANCE OF THE PAINTED MAIDENS

I

AFTER SHE had set sail after she had set sail
After the mother-of-the-earth had set sail

After the earth-mother on her homeward journey,

The fires at the rear of her the fires of the end
The flaming rainbow behind her like a wolf she devours;

Like a manatee strikes down the waters of the beginning

The going the gone-waters the back-swirling eddies
The waves in battle ahead of her in the attacking storm . . .

II

AND THEY came to us after she had set sail
    bringing to us the secret;
And they came bringing to us the secret on
    broken clay tablet cooled . . .

From the seven quarters of the globe,
Past the seven seas past the seven

Distant deserts, bearing beads of coral and
    kolanuts fit for a queen,
They came bringing to us the secret by Man-
    of-Giant-Testicles coded . . .

The gatekeepers at the seven gates heard them,
   trembled at their approach;
The onlookers marvelled at their standards,
   and at their plumed helmets . . .

And they surged round about us and round
   about the clearing,
Round about us like a fence of thorns raised
   against the onlookers . . .

III

FOR IT IS you, shower of rain after drought,
   that we have waited
Menses after menses, without antimony without
   bracelets; while you swam
Diver of centuries, your longest journey, the sea
   of ten thousand leagues . . .

And in your honour, Princess-out-of-exile, the tamarinds
   spread their velvet coverlets,
And our cymbals our calabashes comb the night for the
   alligator hidden in the rushes.

In reverence to your shores, O abyss of wonders,
   our fingers
Tremble above the altar, and the incense smokes
   in the censer;
And eyes of us that have looked on oceans tremble
   before your lagoon . . .

IV

FOR YOU return to us
From a forgotten farewell
From the settled abyss
Where the twilights cross

Several seasons ago
We brought you camwood
Votaries of an ideal
Without age or name

We fed like prayers
Into your memory
Vegetable offerings
Eggs of white hens

Yesterday was Remembrance
Day at the Cathedral
We called you to witness
Involved you in our vows

We did not know you
Who were whom we hold
For to know you was
To know the infinite

Today on your homecoming
Patient mother
With you in our palm
The life hour is our cup

The secret the clay
All the world's farewells
Break behind us
Like wavelash on sandbank.

PATH OF THUNDER:
POEMS PROPHESYING WAR

THUNDER CAN BREAK

FANFARE of drums, wooden bells: iron chapter;
And our dividing airs are gathered home.

This day belongs to a miracle of thunder;
Iron has carried the forum
With token gestures. Thunder has spoken,
Left no signatures: broken

Barbicans alone tell one tale the winds scatter.

Mountain or tower in sight, lo, your hostages –
Iron has made, alas, masterpieces –
Statuettes of legendary heroes – iron birds
Held – fruit of flight – tight;

For barricaded in iron handiwork a miracle caged.

Bring them out we say, bring them out
Faces and hands and feet,
The stories behind the myth, the plot
Which the ritual enacts.

Thunder can break – Earth, bind me fast –
Obduracy, the disease of elephants.

ELEGY OF THE WIND

WHITE LIGHT, receive me your sojourner; O milky way,
   let me clasp you to my waist;
And may my muted tones of twilight
Break your iron gate, the burden of several centuries,
   into twin tremulous cotyledons . . .

Man of iron throat – for I will make broadcast with
   eunuch-horn of seven valves –
I will follow the wind to the clearing,
And with muffled steps seemingly out of breath break
   the silence the myth of her gate.

For I have lived the sappling sprung from the bed
   of the old vegetation;
Have shouldered my way through a mass of ancient
   nights to chlorophyll;

Or leaned upon a withered branch,
A blind beggar leaning on a porch.

I have lived the oracle dry on the cradle of a new generation . . .
The autocycle leans on a porch, the branch dissolves into embers,

The ashes resolve their moments
Of twin-drops of dew on a leaf:
And like motion into stillness is my divine rejoicing –
The man embodies the child
The child embodies the man; the man remembers
The song of the innocent,
Of the uncircumcised at the sight of the flaming razor –

The chief priest of the sanctuary has uttered
   the enchanted words;
The bleeding phallus,
Dripping fresh from the carnage cries out for
   the medicinal leaf . . .

O wind, swell my sails; and may my banner run
   the course of wider waters:

The child in me trembles before the high shelf
   on the wall,
The man in me shrinks before the narrow neck of
   a calabash;

And the chant, already all wings, follows
In its ivory circuit behind the thunder clouds,
The slick route of the feathered serpent . . .

COME THUNDER

NOW THAT the triumphant march has entered the last street
    corners,
Remember, O dancers, the thunder among the clouds . . .

Now that laughter, broken in two, hangs tremulous between
    the teeth,
Remember, O dancers, the lightning beyond the earth . . .

The smell of blood already floats in the lavender-mist of the
    afternoon.
The death sentence lies in ambush along the corridors of
    power;
And a great fearful thing already tugs at the cables of the open
    air,
A nebula immense and immeasurable, a night of deep waters –
An iron dream unnamed and unprintable, a path of stone.

The drowsy heads of the pods in barren farmlands witness it,
The homesteads abandoned in this century's brush fire witness
    it:
The myriad eyes of deserted corn cobs in burning barns witness
    it:

Magic birds with the miracle of lightning flash on their
    feathers . . .

The arrows of God tremble at the gates of light,
The drums of curfew pander to a dance of death;

And the secret thing in its heaving
Threatens with iron mask
The last lighted torch of the century . . .

HURRAH FOR THUNDER

WHATEVER happened to the elephant –
Hurrah for thunder –

The elephant, tetrarch of the jungle:
With a wave of the hand
He could pull four trees to the ground;
His four mortar legs pounded the earth:
Wherever they treaded,
The grass was forbidden to be there.

Alas! the elephant has fallen –
Hurrah for thunder –

But already the hunters are talking about pumpkins:
If they share the meat let them remember thunder.

The eye that looks down will surely see the nose;
The finger that fits should be used to pick the nose.

Today – for tomorrow, today becomes yesterday:
How many million promises can ever fill a basket . . .

If I don't learn to shut my mouth I'll soon go to hell,
I, Okigbo, town-crier, together with my iron bell.

ELEGY FOR SLIT-DRUM

(With rattles accompaniment)

CONDOLENCES . . . from our swollen lips laden with
    condolences:

The mythmaker accompanies us
The rattles are here with us

condolences from our split-tongue of the slit drum condolences

one tongue full of fire
one tongue full of stone –

condolences from the twin-lips of our drum parted in
    condolences:

the panther has delivered a hare
the hare is beginning to leap
the panther has delivered a hare
the panther is about to pounce –

condolences already in flight under the burden of this century:

parliament has gone on leave
the members are now on bail
parliament is now on sale
the voters are lying in wait –

condolences to caress the swollen eyelids of bleeding mourners.

the cabinet has gone to hell
the timbers are now on fire
the cabinet that sold itself
ministers are now in gaol –

condolences quivering before the iron throne of a new
        conqueror:

the mythmaker accompanies us (*the Egret had come and gone*)
Okigbo accompanies us the oracle enkindles us
the Hornbill is there again (*the Hornbill has had a bath*)
Okigbo accompanies us the rattles enlighten us –

condolences with the miracle of sunlight on our feathers:

The General is up . . . the General is up . . . commandments . . .
the General is up the General is up the General is up –

condolences from our twin-beaks and feathers of condolences:

the General is near the throne
an iron mask covers his face
the General has carried the day
the mortars are far away –

condolences to appease the fever of a wake among tumbled
        tombs

the elephant has fallen
the mortars have won the day
the elephant has fallen
does he deserve his fate
the elephant has fallen
can we remember the date –

Jungle tanks blast Britain's last stand –

the elephant ravages the jungle
the jungle is peopled with snakes
the snake says to the squirrel
I will swallow you
the mongoose says to the snake
I will mangle you
the elephant says to the mongoose
I will strangle you

thunder fells the trees cut a path
thunder smashes them all – condolences . . .

THUNDER that has struck the elephant
the same thunder should wear a plume – condolences

a roadmaker makes a road
the road becomes a throne
can we cane him for felling a tree – condolences . . .

THUNDER that has struck the elephant
the same thunder can make a bruise – condolences:

we should forget the names
we should bury the date
the dead should bury the dead – condolences

from our bruised lips of the drum empty of condolences:

trunk of the iron tree we cry *condolences* when we break,
shells of the open sea we cry *condolences* when we shake . . .

ELEGY FOR ALTO

(With drum accompaniment)

AND THE HORN may now paw the air howling goodbye . . .

For the Eagles are now in sight:
Shadows in the horizon –

THE ROBBERS are here in black sudden steps of showers, of
     caterpillars –

THE EAGLES have come again,
The eagles rain down on us –

POLITICIANS are back in giant hidden steps of howitzers, of
     detonators –

THE EAGLES descend on us,
Bayonets and cannons –

THE ROBBERS descend on us to strip us of our laughter, of our
     thunder –

THE EAGLES have chosen their game,
Taken our concubines –

POLITICIANS are here in this iron dance of mortars, of
     generators –

THE EAGLES are suddenly there,
New stars of iron dawn;

So let the horn paw the air howling goodbye . . .

O mother mother Earth, unbind me; let this be
    my last testament; let this be
The ram's hidden wish to the sword the sword's
    secret prayer to the scabbard —

THE ROBBERS are back in black hidden steps of detonators —

FOR BEYOND the blare of sirened afternoons, beyond
    the motorcades;
Beyond the voices and days, the echoing highways; beyond
        the latescence
Of our dissonant airs; through our curtained eyeballs,
    through our shuttered sleep,
Onto our forgotten selves, onto our broken images;
    beyond the barricades
Commandments and edicts, beyond the iron tables,
    beyond the elephant's
Legendary patience, beyond his inviolable bronze
    bust; beyond our crumbling towers —

BEYOND the iron path careering along the same beaten track —

THE GLIMPSE of a dream lies smouldering in a cave,
    together with the mortally wounded birds.
Earth, unbind me; let me be the prodigal; let this be
    the ram's ultimate prayer to the tether . . .

AN OLD STAR departs, leaves us here on the shore
Gazing heavenward for a new star approaching;
The new star appears, foreshadows its going
Before a going and coming that goes on forever . . .